THE DEITY OF CHRIST

BRIAN FULLARTON

Published by Hayes Press

Published by HAYES PRESS

The Barn, Flaxlands,

Royal Wootton Bassett,

Swindon, UK,

SN4 8DY

www.hayespress.org

t. +44 (0)1793 850598

e. info@hayespress.org

www.facebook.com/hayespress.org

https://twitter.com/hayespress

FOREWORD

Who is Jesus? That is definitely one of the most important questions that could ever be asked, as the salvation of every human being that has ever lived depends on the answer! It was a live question when Jesus was here 2,000 years ago, and must surely have been in the minds of the writers of what now forms our New Testament. It's an equally true question today. Was He just a good man, or a wise teacher, or was He (and therefore *is* He) actually God?

Almost every world faith has an opinion on the question, as does almost every man in the street. But the focus of this booklet is on what the Bible has to say about Him. It gives abundant Bible references that have a clear implication in reaching confident conclusions about the deity of Christ; and additionally includes some that are capable of varying explanation. In such instances the writer's views are briefly stated, taking the approach generally that the less clear Bible statements are best understood by fitting them within the most clear statements. It is best not to regard an apparent exception as demolishing a general rule!

This booklet is therefore commended to readers in the confident hope that the Holy Spirit will use the information it contains to their blessing.

Michael Elliott

Hayes Press

TABLE OF CONTENTS

1: INTRODUCTION

"You are the Christ, the Son of the living God."

Matthew, in his Gospel account (Matt.16:16), records for us this positive answer given by Peter to our Lord's question: *"But who do you say that I am?"* Peter was not just - as was so often the case - speaking on behalf of the other apostles, because his words have been echoed by all disciples down the subsequent centuries. But is the Son 'divine'?

"Of the Son, he (God) *says, 'Your throne, O God, is forever and ever, the sceptre of uprightness is the sceptre of your kingdom'"* (Heb.1:8).

The writer to the Hebrews, using a quotation from Psalm 45 of which the original writer could not have appreciated the full significance, gives us the answer. God the Father here refers to the Son as *"God"* – so the Son is as divine a person as God is.

These clear attestations to the deity of the Lord Jesus are the bedrock of the Christian faith and of vital importance not only to all born-again believers, but also to the world of sinners to whom the message of the Gospel is directed. Upon this truth hinges the wonder of the work of salvation, whereby God can both grant forgiveness for humanity's sins and at the same time show acceptance of the person who exercises faith in Christ as the one and only sacrifice for those sins.

2: DEITY CONFIRMED BY GOD THE FATHER'S DIVINE DIALOGUE WITH HIS SON

"And a voice came from heaven, 'You are my beloved Son, with you I am well pleased.'"

What a wonderful public affirmation from our great eternal God of the pleasure which his divine Son brought to him while Christ was here on earth! We are indebted to Mark (1:11), and the other synoptic Gospel writers, for recording this incident for us. By opening the heavens at the start of our Lord's public ministry, immediately following his baptism by John, God the Father puts his divine seal of approval on his Son's mission. The value of the long years of patient preparation that the Lord undertook in the obscurity of Nazareth is summed up beautifully in Luke's Gospel: *"And Jesus increased in wisdom and in stature and in favour with God and man"* (Luke 2:52). Little wonder that the Father was moved to tell his Son, *"with you I am well pleased."*

Much later in his ministry, Jesus took three of his closest disciples - Peter, James and John - with him up a high mountain. There, with Moses and Elijah as the only other witnesses, he was transfigured before them, his face shining like the sun. Once again, God spoke from a bright cloud that overshadowed them: *"This is my beloved Son, with whom I am well pleased; listen to him"* (Matt.17:5). We have already mentioned how, in the previous chapter of his Gospel, Matthew had recorded Peter's opinion of Christ's deity as the eternal Son. He now notes how Peter's assertion receives divine endorsement! This time, God has a little more to say to his human audience, adding the injunction: *"listen to him."* This divine command is every bit as relevant to his disciples today as it was to the three apostles who followed him wonderingly down the mountainside. What better way to spend our time - just as his friend Mary of Bethany did (Luke 10:38-42) - than in listening to him?

In our next chapter we will have the opportunity to do so.

3: DEITY CONFIRMED BY THE SON OF GOD'S DIVINE DIALOGUE WITH HIS FATHER

"I and the Father are one."

"Have I been with you so long, and you still do not know me, Philip? Whoever has seen me has seen the Father. How can you say, 'Show us the Father'? Do you not believe that I am in the Father and the Father is in me?" (John 14:9-10).

"Father, the hour has come; glorify your Son that the Son may glorify you" (John 17:1).

Can anyone listening to such words be left in any doubt as to Christ's deity? Later in the same prayer in the upper room as recorded in John 17, Jesus appeals to his Father, on his disciples' behalf, with these heart-warming and uplifting words: *"Holy Father, keep them in your name, which you have given me, that they may be one, even as we are one"* (v.11). Finally, as he draws his prayer to an end, Jesus addresses God as his *"righteous Father"* (v.25). As we reverently eavesdrop on our Lord's prayer, we hear incontrovertible divine proof of Peter's assertion that Jesus is indeed *"The Christ, the Son of the living God."*

"I and the Father are one" (John 10:30), so John records the words the Lord uses in describing his deity to a group of Jews gathered around him in the Temple colonnade. During his discourse, Jesus refers to *"The works that I do in my Father's name"* (John 10:25). Subsequently, in talking about those to whom he

8

has given eternal life, Jesus states, *"My Father, who has given them to me, is greater than all"* (John 10:29).

4: CHRIST - THE DIVINE CREATOR

"In the beginning was the Word, and the Word was with God, and the Word was God ... All things were made through him, and without him was not any thing made that was made."

So John opens his Gospel record (John 1:1,3), presenting first and foremost the case for Christ as the divine Creator.

Genesis is the book of beginnings, and when we turn to the words of Scripture in our English translation we read *"In the beginning, God created the heavens and the earth"* (Gen.1:1).

It is significant that the name of God is plural in form, not singular or dual, so declaring at this very early stage in the written record the plurality of the Godhead – Father, Son, and Spirit. Collectively, as one God in three persons, they act in unison. The verb *"created"* is singular, and being in the perfect tense stresses activity that was carried out decisively and distinctively as a completed action and not one continuing indefinitely.

Again, in verses 26 and 27 of the first chapter of this book, we have the words of the triune God, *"Let us* (plural) *make man in our* (singular) *image, after our likeness."* This is followed by "So God created man in his own image, in the image of God he created him; male and female he created them." These two verses are not at variance with each other. They are stating one and the same thing; one God in three persons working in perfect harmony.

The writer to the Hebrews begins his letter by confirming the same point: "*God ... has spoken to us by his Son ... through whom also he created the world*" (Heb.1:1-2).

All this is corroborated in the New Testament by the apostle John:

> (i) in his Gospel, where he alludes to the Lord Jesus, the Son of God, as "*the Word*" who was there when the work of creation was begun: "*the Word was with God, and the Word was God*" (John 1:1);

> (ii) in his first letter, using the expression "*the word of life*" (1 John 1:1);

> (iii) and in the letter to the seven churches in Asia Minor, speaking of the Lord Jesus as the "*Alpha and the Omega, the first and the last, the beginning and the end*" (Rev.22:13; cp. 21:6).

The apostle Paul in Colossians 1:18, describes the Lord Jesus as "*the beginning*", i.e. not having a beginning himself but being the creator and cause of everything that has a beginning. The writer to the Hebrews reveals God the Father, using direct speech, accrediting the Son with laying the foundation of the earth and the heavens being the work of his hands (Heb.1:10). So when, in Genesis 2:4, we have the expression "*the LORD God*" in connection with the work of creation, it is clear that the Lord Jesus shares possession, as well as the Father and the Spirit, of this title of eminence. In Hebrew, "*the LORD God*" is 'Jehovah Elohim'. The first word conveys God's glory as one who never fails to honour his word, being constantly bound by it, as an irrevocable covenant; the second reveals his absolute authority, undiminished power and inviolable dominion.

5: CHRIST - THE DIVINE SAVIOUR

"The Father has sent his Son to be the Saviour of the world."

These simple words, penned by the apostle John in his first letter (1 John 4:14), summarise perfectly God's plan of salvation and the roles within it executed by Father and Son.

John's theme throughout his correspondence is *"love"* and more especially *"God's love."* This is revealed to its fullest extent in Christ's coming into the world to be the sacrifice for our sins and in the giving of eternal life to us through faith-belief in his only Son, the Saviour of the world. He describes this divine love most beautifully: *"In this the love of God was made manifest among us, that God sent his only Son into the world, so that we might live through him. In this is love, not that we have loved God but that he loved us and sent his Son to be the propitiation for our sins"* (1 John 4:9-10).

John sums up salvation in an unequivocal, if somewhat stark, way towards the end of his letter: *"Whoever has the Son has life; whoever does not have the Son of God does not have life"* (1 John 5:12).

In his letter to the Galatians, Paul defends the truth of justification by grace through faith in Jesus Christ when it was being undermined by Jews who had believed in Christ, but were insisting the works of the law were also necessary as a means of obtaining God's salvation. He writes of the Lord Jesus in those wonderful words we so often hear quoted in worship and thanksgiving: "*the Son of God, who loved me and gave himself for me*" (Gal.2:20).

If it is unnecessary for a person seeking salvation to believe that Christ is God, why then do we find such statements as the Lord made in Matthew 9:6 where he is shown to have the authority and power to forgive sins; and in Mark 2:6-7,10 which notes that even the Scribes and Pharisees acknowledged that only God could forgive sins (see also Luke 5:21,24)?

6: CHRIST'S DEITY FURTHER DISCLOSED IN THE GOSPELS

Proof abounds in the Gospel records of the position the Lord Jesus occupies in the Godhead as "*The Son.*"

Starting chronologically with **Matthew's** Gospel, very early on we have the visit of an angelic being to Joseph, betrothed to Mary who was chosen to bear the Son of God into this world by natural birth. He declared that the child who was already in her womb at the time of his communication, conceived by the direct involvement of the Holy Spirit, was none other than "*Immanuel*" meaning "*God with us.*" His deity is established irrevocably at the outset of the good news to humankind (Matt.1:18-23).

Satan, the adversary, was in no doubt as to who the Lord Jesus was, readily acknowledging the Lord's ability to perform what would humanly be considered as miraculous acts in turning stones into bread and trying by every means possible to break the Lord's utter dependence on his heavenly Father during his days on earth (Matt.4:3-10). Demons, being agents of the Devil, likewise unreservedly acknowledged the Saviour to be the Son of God who was able, by his word, to consign them to summary punishment (Matt.8:28-33).

Witnessing his complete authority over the wind and waves, the Lord's disciples were quick to confess "*Truly you are the Son of God*" (Matt.14:33). Peter, so often the spokesman for the twelve, when questioned by the Lord as to his true identity, had no hesitation in declaring him to be "*the Christ, the Son of the living*

15

God" (Matt.16:15). He certainly is both Saviour and God. The very fact that the Lord responded to his disciple with the words *"Blessed are you, Simon Bar-Jonah! For flesh and blood has not revealed this to you, but my Father who is in heaven"* demonstrates the Lord's own endorsement of Peter's statement of his deity (Matt.16:17).

On the occasion of two of the disciples being sent to fetch the donkey and colt that had been specially set aside for Christ's entry into the city of Jerusalem, they were instructed to say if questioned about their actions, *"The Lord needs them"* and so he revealed himself to be God in using this title of deity (Matt.21:3).

Even a Roman centurion and his squad of soldiers who were trying to bring the crucifixion proceedings to an orderly end, having seen the earthquake and quickly going over in their minds the events of the day, were impelled to say loudly and with conviction, *"Truly this was the Son of God!"* (Matt.27:54).

Mark begins his account *"The beginning of the gospel of Jesus Christ, the Son of God"* - that is, God's good news that comes with his Son. Christ's deity is soon evidenced in the outburst of a demon-possessed man in the Capernaum synagogue, *"I know who you are – the Holy One of God."* The Lord, in his grace, immediately expels the evil spirit (Mark 1:24).

We do not know the background of the man who was cured of paralysis, but it is significant that the first words spoken by the Lord to him were *"Son, your sins are forgiven"* (Mark 2:5). He then commanded the sufferer to get on his feet, lift up his bed and walk. Unspoken critics sitting and watching what was going on in the house were thinking *"Why does this man speak like that? He is blaspheming! Who can forgive sins but God alone?"* The Lord saw into their hearts and said *"The Son of Man has authority on earth to forgive sins,"* confirming that he is also the Son of God with the right to exercise divine power (Mark 2:3-12).

Our Lord states unequivocally, when he is asked the direct question by the high priest during his interrogation before the Council: *"Are you the Christ, the Son of the Blessed?"* having hitherto remained silent: *"I am, and you will see the Son of Man seated at the right hand of Power, and coming with the clouds of heaven"* (Mark 14:61-62).

Adding to the detail in Matthew's narrative, in **Luke** we have an angelic messenger named Gabriel coming to Mary, Joseph's future wife, announcing that the child she would produce would be a son who would be called *"the Son of the Most High"* (Luke 1:32). Clearly, Gabriel was referring to the Son of God, who is none other than God the Son. On hearing this astounding news, and also that her elderly relative Elizabeth was carrying a child, Mary hurriedly visited her. Recognising Mary's voice at the door, Elizabeth was conscious of her six-month-old baby leaping in the womb for joy, and referred to Mary as the *"mother of my Lord"* (Luke 1:43). We wonder what conversations were had by these two women during their three months together (Luke 1:26-45).

Some of the incidents where the Lord's deity is documented by Matthew and Mark are corroborated by Luke, such as the temptations, testimony of demon spirits and healing of the man with the spinal disorder (see Luke 4:3, 9, 34, 41; 5:21; 8:28, 39).

The opening statement of the Gospel of **John** leaves us in no doubt as to the deity of Christ – He is *"the Word"* (Gk. *'ho logos'* – the full, intelligent expression of all that God is and wishes to communicate to us in and through the person of the Son), mentioned three times in succession in verse one of chapter 1, emphasising his pre-incarnate existence. Moreover, he was **with** (Gk. preposition *'pros'* - in effect always with his face directly set towards the Father) God; and **was** (Gk. verb *'en'* – always being so) God. Later, in verse 14, John confirms the divine action that took place in Christ's incarnation.

Early in our Lord's ministry, some of his followers decided to stop accompanying him on his journeys, finding it difficult to understand his words when he discussed with some Jews what he meant by eating his flesh and drinking his blood (John 6:52-58). Peter, however, was quick to dismiss any idea that those who were among the first to join him would similarly desert him, by saying *"Lord, to whom shall we go? … we have believed, and have come to know, that you are the Holy One of God"* (John 6:68-69).

More than once, the Lord Jesus asserts his oneness in Godhead - equality with the Father, essentially and absolutely one in possession of deity, but altogether separate and distinct in personalities, yet acting in perfect unity. Examples are in John chapter 17:11,22 and 24. In saying *"I and the Father are one"* (John 10:30) the Jews knew exactly who he was claiming to be, as evidenced by their lifting up stones to kill him, saying *"you, being a man, make yourself God"* (John 10:33). Before Pilate, his accusers made the same allegation, *"He ought to die because he has made himself the Son of God"* (John 19:7).

Another verification of the Lord's co-equality with the Father is found in his repeated phrase "*The Father is in me, and I am in the Father,*" spoken to his enemies, his disciples and also directly to his Father in intercession for his own. All the transcendent glory of deity was shared by Father and Son, and Spirit too (Luke 24:33, 36-40; John 10:38; 14:10-11; 17:5, 21; cp. 2 Cor. 3:18; 1 Pet. 4:14).

We cannot leave John's wonderful treatise without mentioning the outburst of praise from the lips of the startled Thomas who had been absent when the Lord had first shown himself to the frightened group in Jerusalem. On seeing his Master's scars, he exclaimed: "*My Lord and my God!*" (John 20:19-20, 24-28).

7: APPEARANCES OF THE LORD JESUS TO PEOPLE IN THE OLD TESTAMENT ('THEOPHANIES')

While we must be cautious in inferring into Scripture what it does not explicitly state, we may suggest with some confidence the appearance on earth of the Lord Jesus Christ, before his incarnation, in a number of Old Testament incidents, given the characteristics of the person described. We thus put forward the following examples for consideration:

To Abraham

Genesis chapter 18 describes how three men appeared before Abraham as he sat by his tent door one day. This encounter took place shortly after the news was broken to him that his elderly wife Sarah would produce a son in her old age; news which caused the man described as God's friend (Jas.2:23) to chortle! It seems that one of them is recognised by him as the "*Lord*" (v.3), obviously appearing in human form. Abraham pleaded with him to spare the city of Sodom (Gen.18: 2-3, 25, 27, 30, 32). Was this none other than the Lord Jesus, into whose hand all judgement is placed as ordained by the Father (see chapter 15 below, Christ - the Divine Judge, especially John 5:22 and Acts 17:31)?

To Moses

On more than one occasion Moses is described in Scripture as "*the man of God*." In Exodus chapter 3, we have an account of the Lord manifesting himself to this wonderfully faithful servant of the Lord: *"The angel of the LORD appeared to him in a flame of fire out of the midst of a bush"* (Ex.3:2). The subsequent narrative describing the 'burning bush' incident on the mountainside would seem to support the view that this *"angel of the Lord"* was none other than the Lord Jesus, on this occasion fully identifying himself as God, who also reveals himself as *"I AM WHO I AM,"* which is literally 'I AM WHO I WILL BE' (Ex.3:13-14). The Hebrew tense emphasises continuance (which can be in the past, present, or future form); consequently, here it is saying 'I continue to be, and will be, who or what I continue to be, and will be.' In simply saying *"I AM"* (Heb. *(EHYEH)*, literally 'I will be', its meaning and thrust seem to denote 'I that ever will be' – in other words, *'The Ever Self-existing One.'*

On the other hand, the Lord clearly informed his servant that he himself would personally stand upon the rock which Moses was instructed to strike with his rod, so that water would flow from it to quench the thirst of his people at that time in their wilderness journey (Ex.17:5-6). This event was foreshadowing the day when the Lord Jesus would be stricken at Calvary by the hand of God as a result of and for our sins, and it is evident on this occasion that the Lord was not seen in angelic or human form. Sadly, Moses on a later occasion struck the rock twice, contrary to the Lord's command, so destroying the typical significance of the once-for-all sacrifice of Christ (see Isa.53:4; Zech.13:7; Num.20:10-13; Heb.10:10,12).

We read in the New Testament of Christ as *"the spiritual Rock"* that followed Israel through the wilderness (1 Cor.10:4). This perhaps suggests that it was the Lord Jesus himself who allowed

Moses to view his back as he passed him by concealed in the cleft of the rock, upon which Moses was told to stand to see his glory (Ex.33:17-23). One day, on earth, the Saviour's back would be lacerated by the whips of the Roman torturers as they scourged him prior to his execution (see Matt.27:26; cf. Isa.50:6).

To Gideon

As with Moses, the one who appeared to Gideon in the guise of an angelic being with a physical presence and form would seem to have been the Lord Jesus, the Son of God. Gideon was chosen by God, yet to others (and in his own assessment) he appeared as a very unlikely soon-to-be deliverer of his people. He later addressed this being, who approached him while he was sitting under an oak tree, as *"Lord"*, and further on as *"Lord God"*, presenting unquestionable proof that it was none other than a divine person confronting him. In acknowledgement of this great privilege, he constructed an altar to the Lord, calling it *"The LORD is Peace"* (Jdgs.6:24; see also 6:11, 15 and 22).

To the parents of Samson

It was the unnamed mother of Samson to whom the angel of the Lord came announcing her forthcoming pregnancy and the way she was to rear her son. As the narrative unfolds in Judges chapter 13, she tells her husband Manoah of this experience, identifying her heavenly messenger/visitor as, *"A man of God"* (v.6). Her husband entreats the Lord for the man of God to come a second time - which he does, but again only to her. She rushes to tell her husband and together they hasten back to the field where he appeared to her. He asks the angel of the Lord his name, to which the reply is given, "*Why do you ask my name, seeing it is wonderful?*" (Jdgs.13:18).

Is it simply coincidental that this same masculine noun, arising from the Hebrew word '*pala*' (the basic meaning of which is 'to be distinguished and extraordinary', and capable of carrying out the most amazing deeds), reappears in the writings of Isaiah in his prophecy of the coming of the Son of God into the world (Isa.9:6)? Surely not. A little later on, after offering a sacrifice of thanksgiving for a son the Lord was going to give them, Manoah said "*we have seen God*" (Jdgs.13: 22).

To Daniel's three friends

Many have speculated as to the identity of the fourth man seen walking with Shadrach, Meshach and Abednego in the fiery furnace. King Nebuchadnezzar describes him *as "like a son of the gods"* (Dan.3:25). Would this not be the Lord Jesus himself, appearing in human form to support these three faithful servants of the Lord?

Other examples

Another instance of the Lord Jesus' deity being attested to is seen in the designation "The LORD" (used three times) that Aaron and his sons had to pronounce as a blessing, as instructed by Moses, upon the people of Israel (Num.6:24-26).

As an aside, we are told it was a "*man of God*" who came to Eli the priest in the days of the judges of Israel. From the use of the language, this is not an instance of a theophany. Two references are given of what God said would happen shortly; firstly

"*Thus the LORD has said,*" and then "*Therefore the LORD, the God of Israel, declares...*" So, it is clear this was a special messenger sent by the Lord, possibly a prophet, but not the Lord himself (1 Sam.2:27, 30).

8: GOD'S REVELATION TO HIS SERVANT JOB AND CHRIST'S DEITY REVEALED IN THE PSALMS

Job

The well-known words of Job *"For I know that my Redeemer lives"* (Job 19:25), immortalised in George Frideric Handel's 'Messiah', give a profound insight into his faith and assurance of one day seeing his Saviour with his own eyes. He knew the day of death would come and his body would turn to dust in the grave, yet was convinced of his own bodily resurrection and the renewal of physical sight, eagerly anticipating that future time (Job 19:25-27). Who else can be identified as Job's (and our) Redeemer than our own Lord Jesus Christ? As Paul reminds us in his letter to Colossians, he is the one *"in whom we have redemption, the forgiveness of sins"* (Col. 1:14).

Psalms

One of the ways to identify the Lord Jesus readily as the subject of prophetic statements in the Old Testament, and particularly in the Psalms, is to discover their appearance in New Testament quotations. The first instance is in the **second Psalm** (vv.1-2) which is quoted virtually verbatim in Acts 4:25-26. The context is the prayer meeting, attended by the apostles Peter and John recently released from custody, in one of the companies of believers meeting together as part of the Church of God in Jerusalem. They have no hesitation in speaking of the *"Lord and against his*

Anointed" as God's holy servant Jesus, who is also "*the Son*" of the psalm, to be acknowledged and revered (see Ps.2:12).

In the same psalm we read the words "*I will tell of the decree: the LORD said to me, 'You are my Son; today I have begotten you'*" (Ps.2:7). This direct speech is surely from the lips of the Saviour himself, rejoicing fully in all that he means to his Father. The same words are found in Hebrews 1:5 in relation to the excellence of his name; in Acts 13:33 in connection with his resurrection; and in Hebrews 5:5 highlighting his priestly service.

Peter, on the day of Pentecost, preaching boldly in Jerusalem to the multitudes of Jews, pilgrims and proselytes of different nationalities, freely quotes **Psalm 16** (vv.8-11). He thereby declares that the words of David, Israel's illustrious king, are nothing less than prophetic with regard to the Lord Jesus' experience in the tomb (where his body would not be allowed to be subject to natural decay) and to his resurrection. Paul also, in the Jewish synagogue in Antioch of Pisidia, quotes directly from the same psalm. Both Peter and Paul were quick to emphasise that what was written (all those nine or so centuries before) was only true of Christ and **not** of David (Acts 2:25-33; 13:35-37).

Psalm 22 is like no other, going to the heart of the Lord Jesus' sufferings on the cross – the physical pain and anguish of crucifixion and the suffering of his soul in bearing God's punishment for our sins, heightened by the cry of dereliction and abandonment (vv.1-2, 19-20). Sufferings change to glory in verse 22: the delight of the Son in honouring his Father to and among those he has justified and sanctified by his precious blood (Heb.2:11-12).

Further thoughts of what our Lord would go through before, during and after the cross are brought out in **Psalm 69**. Undoubtedly David must have gone through many harrowing times in his own life, but the force and depth of the ordeals described could only be realised in their full intensity by the Lord Jesus (see vv.1-4, 9, 14-15, 20-21, 26).

Psalm 110 leaves us in no doubt that the Lord Jesus alone is the answer to any question about the identity of the second "*Lord*" in the first verse, part of which is quoted in Hebrews 1:13. His priesthood, which is spoken of in verse 4, is quoted in Hebrews 5:6. Finally, the Lord's exaltation to glory and his position on the throne of deity at the Father's right hand (Heb.1:3) corresponds to the opening statement in Psalm 110:5.

9: CHRIST'S DEITY REVEALED IN THE PROPHETS

Isaiah

The writings of Isaiah span a period of some 25-30 years, from around 740 - 697 B.C. Four kings of Judah - Uzziah, Jotham, Ahaz and Hezekiah - were the beneficiaries of his presence and power in the land, and his prophecies reveal the most amazing insights into the glories of the person and work of the Lord Jesus. No other Old Testament source is quoted as often in the New Testament as this princely preacher of Christ.

Early on in his service he was shown a heavenly vision of the Lord of hosts – on the throne of eternity, the object of the worship of those high angelic beings, the seraphim: *"Holy, holy, holy is the LORD of hosts; the whole earth is full of his glory!"* (Isa.6:1-3), the ascription of praise to and acknowledgment of a thrice holy triune God. John the apostle informs us in his Gospel that Isaiah saw in this vision his glory and spoke of him, i.e. the Saviour (John 12:41). The prophet also heard the Lord speaking directly to him, *"Whom shall I send, and who will go for us?"* (Isa.6:8). This, surely, provides confirmation once more of the truth of one God in a plurality of three persons.

In the sign given to King Ahaz, the virgin birth is foretold: *"Behold, the virgin shall conceive and bear a son, and shall call his name Immanuel"* (Isa.7:14), meaning, 'God with us.' Later, he is spoken of as *"a son ... given,"* who, among other titles, is also *"Mighty God"* and *"Everlasting Father"* (Isa.9:6). He is also the servant of the LORD (Isa.42:1), whose words of counsel, comfort, and encouragement would lift up the disheartened. Yet ultimately he would be treated as a criminal, being scourged by callous soldiers and smitten, stricken of God, and afflicted for transgressors and sinners like you and me (Isa.53:4-6; see also Matt.27:26; John 19:1).

Micah

The announcement of the Lord's birthplace as Bethlehem was made by Micah the prophet, writing at around the same time period as Isaiah (Mic.5:2). The one of whom he speaks prophetically as the judge of Israel who would be struck with a rod upon the cheeks (Mic.5:1) is the coming ruler in Israel whose activities and movements were not only "*of old*" but also "*from everlasting*" (Mic.5:2, RV). Surely he can only be identified as the Lord Jesus, Israel's true and only Messiah (see also Matt.2:4-6; 27:30)?

Zechariah

Some two centuries later, another prophet named Zechariah spoke of the "*LORD of hosts.*" This is one of the names equally shared as we have seen by Father, Son and Spirit, and also used when only one of the three is speaking. Zechariah writes (Zech.13:7) of the sword being awakened out of its scabbard to strike "*against my shepherd, against the man who stands next to me*" ('is my fellow', RV). I believe that this can be nothing other than a direct reference to the Lord Jesus (cp. Heb.13:20), the same person who will reign in Jerusalem, worshipped by all as "*the King, the LORD of hosts*" (Zech.14:16).

10: CHRIST'S DEITY REVEALED IN ACTS, ROMANS AND CORINTHIANS

Although the word "*lord*" is used in different ways in the Bible to convey the idea of authority at many levels, the biblical title of "*the Lord*" pertains to Deity alone. Peter the apostle freely cited the words of David, king of Israel, in his public address to the crowd gathered in Jerusalem to celebrate the day of Pentecost, and emphasised their importance as being prophetic of God's exaltation of his Son to his side: *"The LORD said to my Lord, 'Sit at my right hand, until I make your enemies your footstool'"* (Ps.110:1). Even though written a millennium before Christ came into the world as a human being, the first six words of this quotation in effect tell us that these are the words spoken by the Father to the Son on the completion of his Cross-work (Acts 2:34).

Saul of Tarsus - on his warhorse, so to speak - heading for Syria's capital and desperate to imprison and even put to death followers of Christ, was blinded by a heavenly light: on hearing a voice asking a reason for his murderous mission, he answered *"Who are you, Lord?"* He knew this was no mere human voice; it had a divine authority. He was correct, as it was indeed Jesus, the Son of God, whom he would later proclaim as such in the synagogues of Damascus (Acts 9:1-5, 19-20; see also 22:8; 26:15).

The Gospel of God, for which the apostle Paul described himself as being "*set apart*," has as its very foundation the Lord's glorious deity as well as his sinless humanity. He is the Son of God who possesses the former, and the son of David regarding the latter. Only through the death of the Son can sinners be released from the sentence and prospect of eternal judgement and be reconciled to God. He is the Christ who is designated *"God over all, blessed forever"* (Rom.9:5) and is worthy of eternal praise and glory on account of his victory on Calvary over Satan, sin and death (Rom.1:1, 3-4; 5:10; 8:1).

Let's now focus on what we will call a church or assembly setting. People in Corinth, a strategic city in southern Greece, who embraced the testimony of Christ heralded by three evangelists - Paul, Silvanus and Timothy - were baptized soon afterwards, and met together to form the Church of God in Corinth. In so doing they became part of what was already known throughout a good part of the Middle East as *"the Way"* - a term appropriately describing a movement begun by the apostles under God, dedicated to teaching the way of the Lord for believers to follow. Though geographically separated from fellow-believers in what were known as 'Churches of God', they were to acknowledge and appreciate the faithfulness of God through whom they were called into *"the fellowship of his Son, Jesus Christ our Lord"* (1 Cor.1:9; see also 1:6; 2 Cor.1:19; Acts 9:2; 18: 8, 25-26).

11: CHRIST'S DEITY REVEALED IN GALATIANS, PHILIPPIANS AND COLOSSIANS

As opposed to writing to single Churches of God, in cities of present-day Italy and Greece (Rome and Corinth, as we have seen above), Paul the apostle sends one letter for circulation around several Churches in the Galatian district of Asia Minor (now Turkey), where there were at least twelve identified Churches of God. They were under attack from the adversary, who was promoting a perversion of the Gospel. Paul quickly establishes his credentials as one who was divinely called to preach the Gospel, revelling in the working of God in his life right from the beginning and later on, as we have witnessed, being called by God's grace and the revelation of "*his Son*" (Gal.1:11, 15-16).

Again, in writing to believers in the Church of God in Philippi, Paul appeals for unity both in the teaching of divine truth and in appropriate behaviour as testimony to the world around them. Humility was brought to the forefront in his encouragement to give careful thought to the mind-frame of Christ Jesus, "*who, though he was* (and ever is) *in the form of God, did not count equality with God a thing to be grasped*" (Phil.2:6). The Lord Jesus is co-equal, co-existent and co-eternal with the Father and the Spirit. He is a full sharer in deity without having to assert it.

One of the most expressive and endearing titles of the Lord Jesus – "*the Son of his* (God's) *love*" – is found in another of the apostle's writings to an individual Church of God - this time in Colossae, an inland town in the south-western part of present-day Turkey (Col.1:13, RV). In its heyday it was regarded as one of the most important cities in the province, but sadly in New Testament times it found itself in the economic doldrums. What could not be taken away from it was the tremendous impact of the Gospel of Jesus Christ.

Paul goes right back to who Christ actually was and ever is, describing him as *"the image of the invisible God, the first-born* (Gk. *'prototokos'* meaning 'before') *of all creation"* (Col.1:15). All that God is essentially and intrinsically, Christ is also because he is nothing other and nothing less than very God himself - who delivers all who believe on him from the realm of darkness, reconciling them in the process to God. More than that, the same deliverer is the one in whom *"all the fullness of God was pleased to dwell"* in his human form – combining deity and humanity in one Person (Col.1:19; see also 1:21-22; 2:9).

12: CHRIST'S DEITY REVEALED IN THE PASTORAL LETTERS

When writing the first of his letters to a younger man called Timothy whom he highly regarded, Paul in his acclamation to *"the King of ages, immortal, invisible, the only God, be honour and glory forever and ever"* (1 Tim.1:17) refers, in the opinion of the present writer, to the Person of the Lord Jesus. My reasoning is that the word for *immortal* in the ESV is the Greek word *'apharthosi'* meaning 'not corruptible', and is related to the fact of the Lord's body not being subjected to corruption (see Acts 2:27,31).

Additionally, in the preceding verses (1 Tim.1:12-16) there is so much said about the amazing work of Christ in Paul's life that it would seem inconsistent for Paul to be referring to anyone else. Further evidence of his deity is later adduced near the end of this letter to his fellow-worker, when he refers to Christ at the time of his appearing as *"the blessed and only Sovereign, the King of kings and Lord of lords, who alone has immortality, who dwells in unapproachable light, whom no one has ever seen or can see. To him be honour and eternal dominion. Amen"* (1 Tim.6:15-16; see also Rev.19:16).

Titus, another close co-worker of Paul's, is the recipient of a most wonderful letter from the aged apostle's hand, referring among other matters to the return from heaven of the Lord Jesus for his own. This event is to be highly anticipated and is a superbly motivational factor for Christians living in an ungodly world. It is called *"our blessed hope, the appearing of the glory of our great God and Saviour Jesus Christ*" (Tit.2:13). This surely provides yet another testimony to his unquestionable possession of deity.

13: TESTIMONY TO THE LORD'S DEITY IN THE LETTER TO THE HEBREWS

Very clear statements of the Lord Jesus' deity are found right at the start of this letter to Jewish believers, written to confirm that Christ alone is the true foundation and focus of their faith. Reference is made to God's communication in their history through his prophets and the messages they brought from him. But now, at the time of writing and thereafter, God's direct line of contact with the world is through his Son, *"whom he appointed the heir of all things, through whom also he created the world. He is the radiance of the glory of God and the exact imprint of his nature"* (Heb.1:2-3). He is thus the full expression of all that God is in his essential being. The Father speaks intimately and unequivocally to the Son, declaring his eternal being, the relationship they have and enjoy, and the Son's everlasting rule, authority and enthronement (Heb.1:5-8). Further on in the letter, evidence is produced of his calling and induction into a priesthood service - rightly his through the sacrificial work of Calvary - that is so much more personal, empathetic and effective than Israel's priesthood of a bygone era – that of Aaron and his sons (Heb.4:14-15; 5:5-6; 7:11-17, 26-28).

14: THE DEITY OF GOD'S SON REVEALED IN THE BOOK OF REVELATION

We cannot be absolutely certain if it is the Lord Jesus who articulates the august words of Revelation 1:8 "'*I am the Alpha and the Omega,' says the Lord God, 'who is and who was and who is to come, the Almighty,'*" or the Father himself, as he is the divine person who has given to the apostle the revelation of Jesus Christ. Nonetheless, there can be no doubt it is the Saviour who lays his right hand upon his prostrate servant, John, proclaiming "*Fear not, I am the first and the last, and the living one*" (Rev.1:17-18). This title reveals the eternal being of the Son and is undeniable proof once again of his deity.

Of highest importance too is what is being brought out in this vision given to John - the Lord's profound interest in those who belong to him being together in a visible, corporate testimony to his name. Of note too is his surveillance over the golden lampstands, giving encouragement and also admonition where appropriate (chaps. 2 and 3). He occupies the throne of heaven, surrounded by an elevated order of angelic beings who sit upon their own thrones; and then we are introduced to the highest order of angels who are named the "*four living creatures*" (Rev.4:2,4,6). These special creatures ceaselessly give worship to the three persons of the Godhead – Father, Son and Spirit - in their anthem of praise:

"*Holy, holy, holy, is the Lord God Almighty, who was and is and is to come!*" (Rev.4:8).

The closing message of this fascinating book, largely dealing with future events, is from the Lord Jesus himself, assuring us of his soon return (Rev.22:12,20), underwritten by his spoken title of excellence:

"I am the Alpha and the Omega, the first and the last, the beginning and the end" (Rev.22:13).

15: CHRIST - THE DIVINE JUDGE

"The Father judges no one, but has given all judgement to the Son."

John records in his Gospel narrative (John 5:22) this clear statement of our Lord with regard to his own unique role in judgement; a role clearly delegated by God the Father to his Son. Later in this same discourse, Jesus expands the point by explaining, *"I can do nothing on my own. As I hear, I judge, and my judgement is just, because I seek not my own will but the will of him who sent me"* (John 5:30). Who could possibly doubt Christ's deity following such an insight into divine intention regarding judgement?

In his letters, Paul provides further insight into Christ's role as Judge. Firstly, in his letter to the Romans (2:16), he writes: *"On that day when, according to my gospel, God judges the secrets of men by Christ Jesus."* Then, in his second letter to Timothy, he speaks of *"the crown of righteousness, which the Lord, the righteous judge, will award to me on that Day, and not only to me but also to all who have loved his appearing"* (4:8). What a wonderful prospect!

In conclusion, let us consider the words with which John draws 'The Revelation' to an end:

"He who testifies to these things says, 'Surely I am coming soon.' Amen. Come, Lord Jesus!" (Rev.22:20)

Brian Fullarton

Did you love *The Deity of Christ*? Then you should read *Baptism - Its Meaning and Teaching* by Hayes Press!

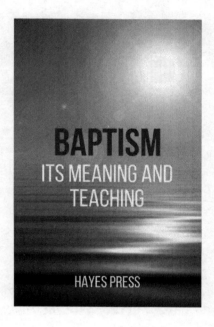

The closing words of the Lord Jesus to the eleven disciples on are all-important for all time.

'And Jesus came and said to them, "All authority in heaven and on earth has been given to me. Go therefore and make disciples of all nations, baptizing them in the name of the Father and of the Son and of the Holy Spirit ..."' (Matt.28:18-19).

This is the Lord's mandate to his apostles to teach and carry out the practice of baptism. This booklet endeavours to explore its relevance, taking a broadly chronological approach to the subject.

About the Publisher

Hayes Press (www.hayespress.org) is a registered charity in the United Kingdom, whose primary mission is to disseminate the Word of God, mainly through literature. It is one of the largest distributors of gospel tracts and leaflets in the United Kingdom, with over 100 titles and hundreds of thousands despatched annually. In addition to paperbacks and eBooks, Hayes Press also publishes Plus Eagles Wings, a fun and educational Bible magazine for children, and Golden Bells, a popular daily Bible reading calendar in wall or desk formats. Also available are over 100 Bibles in many different versions, shapes and sizes, Bible text posters and much more!